TEEN DAYS

Americans All biographies are inspiring life stories about people of all races, creeds, and nationalities who have uniquely contributed to the American way of life. Highlights from each person's story develop his contributions in his special field — whether they be in the arts, industry, human rights, education, science and medicine, or sports.

Specific abilities, character, and accomplishments are emphasized. Often despite great odds, these famous people have attained success in their fields through the good use of ability, determination, and hard work. These fast-moving stories of real people will show the way to better understanding of the ingredients necessary for personal success.

For Sale,
A LIKELY HEALTHY, YO
NEGRO WENCH
BETWEEN twelve and thirteen
she has been used to the Busi-
ness. Sold for want of Employ,
No. 8 Will
Ne Y   1860

Sojourner
Truth

FEARLESS CRUSADER

by Helen Stone Peterson

illustrated by Victor Mays

GARRARD PUBLISHING COMPANY
CHAMPAIGN, ILLINOIS

To Doris

Picture credits:

Library of Congress: pp. 71, 76
Michigan Historical Collections of the University of
    Michigan: p. 92 (bottom)
Schomburg Collection, New York Public Library: pp. 53,
    92 (top)

Contents

1. God in Heaven

"Why is mama working upstairs so late?" Belle asked her father one cold evening in 1806.

"There must be some trouble," the old man replied uneasily. Sick with chills and fever, he lay on some straw on the rough board floor of the cellar that was their home. Here in the Hudson River valley of New York, a Dutchman named Charles Hardenbergh owned a large farm. The fourteen slaves who belonged to him lived in the damp cellar under his big house.

Belle saw that her father was shivering.

"I'll get your medicine, papa," she said in Dutch, the only language she knew. She held her father's head carefully while she gave him the medicine her mother had made from wild roots.

Belle's full name was Isabella, and she was tall for a nine-year-old. Her father was called Bomefree, a Dutch nickname that meant "straight as a tree." By this time, however, the back of the old slave was bent from long years of hard work. He was often sick. He had felt great sorrow too. His first two wives had been sold away from him. His third wife, Mau-Mau Bett, Belle's mother, had had twelve children. However, one by one they were sold away. Now only Belle and her younger brother Peter were left.

Suddenly Belle heard footsteps. She threw a fresh pine log on the fire that supplied both light and heat in the cellar. Mau-Mau Bett entered with Peter, her big hand clutching her son's small one.

"The master is very ill," she burst out. "He's going to die!"

Bomefree moaned, "What will become of us?" The other slaves, who had gathered to hear the news, began to moan too.

Mau-Mau Bett sobbed bitterly. "When the master dies, we'll all be sold." She

turned to Bomefree. "Our last two children will be taken from us."

Belle was terror-stricken. She flung her arms around her mother. "Mama, don't let it happen!" she begged. Belle felt that without her parents she could not go on.

Her father began to mutter. "I knew a master who threw a slave child against a wall and knocked out its brains. An Indian friend of mine said he would have hurled his tomahawk at the murderer's head. He asked me why I didn't kill the master—kill . . ."

"Stop!" ordered Mau-Mau Bett. "The only way we can go on is by trusting God." She turned to Belle and Peter. "Children, if you are separated from us, talk to God. Listen to the answers He gives you. He will help you."

Belle had often heard her mother speak

about God. This evening her words had new importance for the frightened girl. "Mama, tell me where God is," Belle begged.

Mau-Mau Bett led her children outside and pointed to the sky. "God is up there in heaven. Right now He sees all my other children, even though I don't know where they are."

Mau-Mau Bett walked back into the cellar and sat down in a chair. She lifted her son to her lap and drew Belle to her side. Then she began singing African songs her mother had passed down to her. Belle did not understand the words, but she knew some of the songs had happy sounds. Others seemed filled with sorrow. Leaning close against her mother, Belle wept.

Before long, Charles Hardenbergh died.

Soon a sale of his possessions was advertised. The notice read: "Slaves, horses, and other cattle will be sold."

On the morning of the sale, a member of the Hardenbergh family made a grand announcement to Belle's parents. He said, "We have decided to set you both free."

The old couple trembled with joy, for they had longed to be free. It saddened them, however, that their children were not freed too. Actually this sudden freeing of the old slaves saved the Hardenberghs money. Now they would not have to look after Bomefree who was worn out. Mau-Mau Bett would have to support him.

The sale started off well, and Peter and the other slaves brought good prices. Then it was Belle's turn to stand on the wooden platform and be sold. No one bid for her, though. She had a faraway look in her

eyes that made many in the crowd uneasy. "She might not obey," they thought.

The man in charge of the sale shouted, "Get a bargain! Buy this female and I'll throw in a flock of sheep. What will you pay?"

"One hundred dollars," called out John Neely. He was a storekeeper who lived a few miles away. The offer was accepted.

Mr. Neely climbed on his horse and motioned for Belle to walk behind him. Her mother and father came hurrying to say good-bye.

"I'll manage to come see you," Bomefree promised, sobbing.

Tears streamed down Mau-Mau Bett's cheeks. She kissed Belle and whispered, "Talk to God! He will help you."

Mr. Neely rode away. After him trotted the terrified, heartbroken black child.

2. Slave Masters

Mrs. Neely glared at the black girl who followed her husband into the kitchen. "Who's that?" she asked sharply.

"I bought a slave to help you with the housework," her husband answered. The Neelys, who were newcomers in the county, had never before owned a slave.

Mrs. Neely's eyes narrowed. She hated black skin, and this girl's skin was pure black. "What's your name?" she demanded.

Belle stared at her new mistress, not answering.

"She doesn't speak English, only Dutch,"

said Mr. Neely. The Neelys did not speak Dutch.

"John Neely, you must have lost your senses," cried his wife.

"Now the war begins," thought Belle, seeing Mrs. Neely's rage.

Dazed and frightened, Belle did not learn English quickly. When Mrs. Neely sent her for the frying pan, she brought back the kettle. When Mr. Neely sent her to the smokehouse for bacon, she brought back a ham.

One Sunday morning everything went wrong. Mr. Neely ordered Belle to the barn. He tied her hands together, and with a thick switch, he whipped the ten-year-old girl until the blood ran down her legs. She sobbed wildly. Mr. Neely whipped her again. When he left the barn, the girl lay in a pool of her own blood.

16

"I shall get away from here," Belle promised herself, as she struggled to get up.

To her great joy, her father came to see her a few weeks later. Belle managed to leave the house and be alone with him briefly. She showed him the terrible scars from the beating. It had been only one of many. Bomefree could not hold back his bitter tears.

"My poor child, I'll try to find a better master for you," he promised.

Not long afterward Martin Schryver stopped at the house. He was a fisherman who also owned a tavern near the Hudson River. He asked Belle, "Would you like to work for my wife and me?"

"Yes," she replied eagerly. She felt sure her father had told this man about her. Mr. Schryver bought Belle for $105.

The Schryvers had little money, but they were jolly, easygoing people. While Belle was living with them, she learned to speak English though she never did learn to read and write. Belle helped unload the fish from Mr. Schryver's boats. She spent sunny hours hoeing in the garden. She grew strong and tall. By the time she was thirteen years old, she stood among other girls like an oak among saplings.

Mr. John Dumont, who had a large estate at New Paltz, saw Belle. He said he wanted to buy her.

"I'm not selling her," Mr. Schryver told him.

"I'll give you three times what you paid for her," offered Mr. Dumont.

"Oh, my goodness," exclaimed Mrs. Schryver. She begged her husband to sell

Belle. "We don't own anything else that will bring such a nice profit," she pointed out. The sale was soon arranged.

At the Dumonts' Belle helped with the cooking and did the laundry. She worked in the barn and the fields as well. Mr. Dumont, who owned ten slaves, was very pleased with Belle.

"She does more than six ordinary workers," he told his family.

Mrs. Dumont preferred white house-servants, and she had one named Kate. Kate set out to make trouble for the slave girl who had become Mr. Dumont's favorite.

One morning the potatoes that Belle boiled for breakfast looked dirty. "Here's a fine example of Belle's work," snapped Mrs. Dumont.

The potatoes looked dirty a second

morning, and again on a third morning. Frantic with worry, Belle kicked the cat.

"I'll not have you hurting the cat!" shouted Mr. Dumont. He whipped Belle.

Later that day the Dumonts' daughter Gertrude spoke to Belle. "I hate to have the family so angry at you. I'll try to find out what's happening to the potatoes."

The next morning Gertrude took a book and sat by the kitchen fireplace. Belle put the kettle of peeled potatoes over the fire. Then, as usual, she left to help milk the cows. Before long Gertrude saw Kate slip past her and throw ashes into the kettle.

Gertrude ran to her parents. "I know what's been happening to Belle's clean potatoes!" She told the story.

Mrs. Dumont tossed her head, making no comment.

Mr. Dumont exclaimed, "I said Belle is

the best worker we ever had. I plan to give her some special privileges."

One day word came that Mau-Mau Bett was dead. Belle was heartsick at the thought that she would never again hear her beloved mother's voice. Mr. Dumont let her ride to the funeral in one of his farm wagons.

Belle found her old father filled with despair. "I thought I'd go before your mother," he cried, clinging to Belle's hand. "What's to become of me?" Bomefree was now badly crippled and nearly blind.

"If I were free, I'd take care of you, papa," sobbed Belle.

For a time some members of the Hardenbergh family tried to look after Bomefree. Then they sent him to live in a lonely cabin in the woods. He was found there one day, frozen to death.

3. Rebellious Slave

When Belle was in her late teens, she fell in love with a handsome young slave named Bob. He worked on a nearby farm. Although Belle was now almost six feet tall, Bob was even taller.

Bob longed to marry Belle, but Mr. Catlin, his master, would not allow it. He said Bob must marry a slave on the home place. One day Bob told Belle that Mr. Catlin had ordered him not to visit her again. "But I have to see you. And I shall!" declared Bob.

On a Saturday afternoon a few weeks after this, Belle lay sick on her straw bed. The Dumont slaves all slept together in a one-room shed behind the kitchen. Mr. Dumont stepped into the shed.

"Belle, have you seen Bob?"

"No, master," she said.

"If you do, tell him the Catlins are after him," warned Mr. Dumont.

Suddenly Belle heard a commotion outside. She dragged herself to the window. With horror she saw that Mr. Catlin and his son were beating Bob with heavy canes. His face and head were covered with blood. The Catlins kept pounding him.

"Stop!" called Mr. Dumont. "I'll have no slaves killed here."

The Catlins tied Bob with a rope and led him away.

Belle never saw Bob again. He married one of Mr. Catlin's slaves, and a short time later he died.

Belle felt lost and alone. Then she remembered her mother's words. "The only way we can go on is by trusting God," Mau-Mau Bett had said.

"I must have a secret place where I can talk to God," Belle decided.

She knew of a small island in a narrow stream. On this island she made a clearing, then wove branches into a wall around it. Now she had a room where no person could see her. And no person could hear her voice, for the stream fell over some rocks nearby and made a roaring sound.

In this secret place Belle regularly prayed aloud. Fixing her eyes on the sky, she talked to God.

Here, too, in her deep-toned voice, she sang the African songs her mother had passed down to her. The music filled Belle with warmth and pleasure.

She continued to visit her secret place during the rest of her years with the Dumonts. At Mr. Dumont's command she married Tom, a much older slave on the farm. Mr. Dumont had sold away Tom's

two previous wives. Belle had five children
—four daughters and a son.

Now, when Belle worked in the fields,
she took her small children with her. This
way she could watch over them. She carried the baby in a basket that she would
hang on a bush. Then one of Belle's girls
would swing the basket until the baby fell
asleep.

While her children were still small, Belle began looking forward joyously to freedom for all her family. In 1817 New York had passed a law that said adult slaves must be set free on July 4, 1827. Children were to stay and serve their masters— girls to the age of twenty-five and boys to twenty-eight. Then they, too, would be free.

Mr. Dumont made Belle a promise. "You have worked so hard that I'll give your freedom to you one year early." He said Tom could also have his freedom then.

In 1826 Belle hurt her hand badly. She continued to work hard, though. Yet on July 4 Mr. Dumont told her, "You can't have your freedom. You didn't do as much work as usual these past months."

"But, master, you promised!" protested Belle.

"It's settled," Mr. Dumont said. "You won't be free until next year."

"He lied to me," thought Belle, and she reached a decision. "I shall take my freedom." She was now twenty-nine years old.

Belle talked to her husband. Old Tom's heart thumped with fear as he listened to his strong-minded wife. "I'm staying safely here and so should you," he told her.

Belle went to her secret place and prayed. She made her plans. She stayed to help harvest the crops. Then one morning just before daybreak, Belle picked up her baby Sophia and walked off.

A few miles away she stopped at the home of a Quaker family, Mr. and Mrs. Isaac Van Wagener, whom she knew slightly. Like many Quakers the Van

Wageners were against slavery. They received Belle kindly and asked her to stay with them.

Before long Mr. Dumont arrived. "You ran away," he said to Belle.

"No, I took the freedom you promised me," she replied with dignity.

"You must come back," Mr. Dumont ordered.

"No, I shall not," asserted Belle.

Mr. Van Wagener said to Mr. Dumont, "I do not believe in slavery. I will pay what you think is due you, so that Belle and her baby may have their freedom now." Mr. Dumont took twenty-five dollars and left.

Belle started to thank Mr. Van Wagener. "Master . . ."

"Don't call me that," said the gentle Quaker. "You have no master but God."

4. "I'll Have My Child"

Belle lived with the Van Wageners and did their housework. She was lonesome for her older children. However, she thanked God she had her baby Sophia with her. For about a year Belle stayed in the Van Wageners' peaceful, quiet home.

Suddenly one autumn day she had horrible news. She learned that her six-year-old son Peter was a slave on a plantation in the South. Mr. Dumont had sold Peter to his neighbors the Gedneys. But then Solomon Gedney had traded Peter to his brother-in-law in Alabama. Now Peter would not be set free at age twenty-eight, for Alabama had no such arrangement. This sale across state lines was against the law.

"I must get my son back," sobbed Belle.

She left Sophia in the care of the Van Wageners. Then Belle hurried to the Dumonts' farm in New Paltz, running a good part of the way. Mr. Dumont was not at home, but Belle poured out her grief to Mrs. Dumont.

Mrs. Dumont's eyes were filled with hate. "A fine fuss to make about a little black boy!"

Belle's eyes flashed. "I'll have my child again!"

"How?" demanded Mrs. Dumont. "You have no money—nothing."

Belle lifted her head proudly. "God will help me," she said. Later Belle told her friends, "I felt as if the power of a nation was within me."

Belle went to a Quaker family in New Paltz. They said she must take her case to the court in Kingston nine miles away.

At the courthouse in Kingston, Belle talked with an official named Mr. Chip. He drew up a legal paper that ordered Solomon Gedney to appear in court. Mr. Gedney learned about the paper and left at once for Alabama to get Peter.

Belle decided to stay close to the courthouse until Mr. Gedney returned. She earned money by doing housework.

In the spring Mr. Gedney finally came back with Peter. But the next session of court was not till autumn, Mr. Chip told Belle. A panic came over her.

"I must have my son now," protested Belle.

"That's nonsense," snapped Mr. Chip.

Belle walked away from his office, wondering where to turn for help. On the street a stranger stopped her. "Did they give your boy to you?" he asked.

Tears sprang to Belle's eyes as she told him of the delay.

The stranger said, "Listen to me. I feel sure that Lawyer Romeyne can get your son for you now." He pointed out the lawyer's house.

Belle knocked on the door, and Mr. Romeyne himself opened it. He stared at the tall, bare-footed, black woman. "I must talk with you," Belle cried.

"Come in," said Mr. Romeyne gruffly.

Peter's story tumbled from Belle. "All right, I'll get your son," said the lawyer. "But first I need five dollars to pay a man to go to the Gedneys."

34

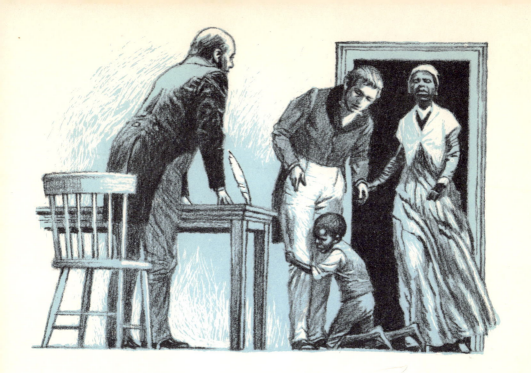

Belle did not have a cent. Once more she walked to New Paltz. Her Quaker friends gave her the money, and she turned it over to Mr. Romeyne. The day after that, Mr. Gedney brought Peter to the courthouse.

When Belle entered the judge's chamber, Peter shouted, "She's not my mother!" Throwing his arms around Mr. Gedney's knees, Peter yelled, "I want to stay with my good master."

The judge saw that there were bad scars on Peter's face. He asked, "What caused that scar on your forehead?"

Peter looked quickly at Mr. Gedney before replying, "A horse kicked me."

Peter was a very frightened boy, the judge realized. He asked more questions and decided that Mr. Gedney had forced the boy to lie. Then he ordered that Peter be given to Belle.

That night when she took off Peter's shirt, Belle saw that his entire back was covered with deep scars. "What's all this?" she asked brokenly.

Peter began to sob. "It's where the master down South whipped and kicked me."

Belle gathered her sobbing son into her arms and hugged him tightly.

Belle continued to work in the Kingston

area. She found a job for Peter at a place where he could live. She longed to have Peter and Sophia with her. The little girl was still at the Van Wageners'. But the only job Belle could get was as a servant with people who had no room for her children. Mr. Dumont felt a bit sorry about what had happened to Peter. So he took Sophia to live on his farm. There she was looked after by her older sisters who had to work for Mr. Dumont until they were twenty-five.

Tom had his freedom now, but no one would give regular work to the old, untrained man. Hunger forced him to enter the poorhouse. There he remained until he died.

It was Belle's great faith in God that brought her through these hard times. She had never been allowed to go to church during her years in slavery. Now she attended the Methodist church in Kingston. Here she became friendly with a New York City schoolteacher named Miss Gear, who spent her vacations in Kingston.

"Peter should have an education," Miss Gear told Belle. Though no school in the area took blacks, Miss Gear told Belle that some schools in New York did. "If you will come to the city, I will pay for Peter's education," Miss Gear said. "And I'll find work for you."

"We shall go," Belle decided.

She was sorry to say good-bye to her daughters. Holding back her tears, Belle told the girls, "Someday I hope to have a home where we all can be together."

5. "The Kingdom"

Belle and Peter moved to New York in 1829. Miss Gear placed the boy in school and found a home for him. She knew a deeply religious family who were pleased to hire Belle to do housework.

This family and their friends often held prayer meetings on street corners. They hoped to turn more people to religion. Belle gladly took part in these services. She was looking for ways to serve God.

During her third year in New York,

Belle became housekeeper for Elijah Pierson, a wealthy widower. Mr. Pierson was a kind person and full of religious zeal.

"God intends to set up His kingdom of love and peace on earth," Mr. Pierson told Belle repeatedly. He spent a great deal of time reading the Bible to her and telling her what it meant. Some of his explanations were strange indeed. He was well known in religious circles for his odd ideas.

One day there was a knock on the door, and Belle answered it. She saw a man with shoulder-length hair and a beard one foot long. He looked just like the pictures of prophets she had seen in the Bible.

"My name is Matthias. I have been sent by God to set up the kingdom of heaven on earth," he said.

"Oh yes!" gasped Belle. The words rang true to her, for Mr. Pierson had prepared her for them.

The fact was that Matthias had been arrested more than once for disturbing the peace. The authorities had thought he was insane, but he convinced them he was not. Now he convinced Mr. Pierson that he was God's messenger. He won other followers too. Among them were Ben Folger, a well-to-do businessman, and his wife.

Belle, Mr. Pierson, and the rest of the followers moved with Matthias to a country estate. They called it "The Kingdom." It was supposed to be a place where all lived and worked in a spirit of brotherly love. However Belle, the only black person in the group, was kept busy at the hard work. Others had light tasks. Matthias did little except enjoy himself and preach some ridiculous sermons. Soon there were jealous quarrels and angry words among his white followers. Love and peace were certainly not present in "The Kingdom," Belle realized.

By this time Mr. Pierson was ill in both mind and body. Belle looked after him the best she could. When he died suddenly, "The Kingdom" broke up. Belle returned to New York.

Relatives of Mr. Pierson said that he

had been poisoned. Matthias was arrested and tried for murder, but was found not guilty. During the trial the Folgers spread the rumor that Belle had tried to poison them.

"An African witch," a newspaperman wrote of Belle. "She is the most wicked of the wicked."

Belle was stunned. Then, gathering her strength, she made up her mind to fight these untruths.

Her first step was to get proof of her good character. She went back to Kingston. Her past employers in that area wrote letters that highly praised her.

While Belle was trying to think what to do next, a rare thing happened. A white newspaperman by the name of Gilbert Vale came forward to help her. He knew she was being treated unfairly.

"People are prejudiced against her because she is black, poor, and uneducated," he said.

Mr. Vale made a complete investigation. Then he wrote a two-volume book in defense of the former slave.

Meanwhile, with great courage, Belle decided to go to court. She started a suit for slander against the prominent Mr. Folger. He had spread lies, she said, that hurt her reputation. At that time most blacks in the United States were still slaves. It was very unusual for a black person to sue a white one. Yet Belle won the case. The all-white jury awarded her a small sum of money for the damage done to her good name. It was a shining triumph for Belle.

The Matthias affair left her a lot wiser. And from then on she never let anyone tell her what the Bible meant. Belle explained, "I talk to God and God talks to me."

Belle stayed in New York doing housework. As the years went by, she grew more and more troubled over her son Peter. He had quit school. Due to his lack of education, he was often jobless. Now he was getting into trouble.

Peter liked ships. When he consented to go to sea as a sailor, Belle was pleased. She received several letters from him. Then the letters stopped, and Belle never heard from her son again. She feared his ship had sunk at sea.

Belle was torn with grief over Peter. "He had no childhood, only beatings," she told herself. Her heart was heavy as she thought of all the cruelty and injustice suffered by black people.

Belle's thoughts turned to her daughters. She had visited them as often as she could. But she had not been able to save money to buy a home where they might live with her. Though Belle worked hard, her employers paid her next to nothing.

In New York Belle had seen many people, both black and white, who were even poorer than she was. They often went hungry, and their homes were miserable. How could such poverty be overcome? And how could cruelty and injustice be done away with?

For Belle the true answer lay in God's command: "Do unto others as you would have them do unto you."

Belle thought and prayed. It came to her that God had new work for her to do. She told a friend, "The Lord has

46

given me a new name—Sojourner. I'm to travel up and down the land, telling people about God's commands."

She packed a few clothes in a pillow-case. Then on a June morning in 1843, Sojourner, now forty-six years old, left New York. She started walking toward Long Island to spread God's word.

6. God's Sojourner

Sojourner moved along with brisk steps. Happily she whispered her new name, "Sojourner."

She had no exact plans. But she told herself firmly, "God has work for me to do ahead, bringing His truth to people." In great excitement she spoke aloud. "Truth! My full name will be Sojourner Truth."

That night she stopped at a house and asked to sleep there. She had no trouble finding places to stay as she continued her journey. Cheerfully she helped with housework or nursing at each stop.

On Long Island and throughout New England, white people were holding religious meetings. Sojourner walked from meeting to meeting, many of which were held outdoors or in tents. Soon she was speaking at them, like a preacher. "To be good in the eyes of God, you must do good to all His children," she would tell the crowds.

By the time Sojourner had reached Springfield, Massachusetts, she was tired. She said to friends, "I'd like to stay awhile in some nice place."

They told her about a cooperative community, or commune, near Northampton, Massachusetts. The members believed in the worth and dignity of every individual.

They lived simply. They supported themselves by raising silkworms and weaving silk cloth.

"I'll go to see this place," Sojourner decided.

Her heart sank when she saw the ugly brick building where the people lived. It housed the silk factory as well. The group gave Sojourner a warm welcome, however, and she decided to stay. She took on the job of washing the clothes for the community.

She soon learned that most of the adults were abolitionists. They demanded that slavery in the South be abolished, or done away with, at once. Abolitionists were a small minority in the nation, and many Americans hated them. Sojourner met the leaders of the movement when they visited the community. She came to know

13974

Frederick Douglass, the escaped slave, who was now lecturing at antislavery meetings.

Sojourner thought, "Does God have work for me to do in freeing the slaves?"

She was still searching for an answer to this question when the community ended. The silk business had not made enough money for the people to live on. Sojourner stayed at Northampton and did housework. One day Olive Gilbert, an abolitionist friend, talked with her.

"People should read of the cruel things you and your family suffered in slavery. Then more of them would be aroused to wipe out this wickedness. Will you talk to me about your life? I will write it down for you in a book."

"Yes, yes!" cried Sojourner. She was certain that God had opened the way for her to help free the slaves.

Miss Gilbert wrote the book. It was published in 1850 when Sojourner was fifty-three. "Start traveling to antislavery meetings," Miss Gilbert advised her. "People there will buy your book and read it. Then they will tell others of the evil of slavery."

Sojourner began attending meetings in Massachusetts. She took along copies of

This picture of Sojourner faced the title page of Miss Gilbert's book about the former slave's sad life.

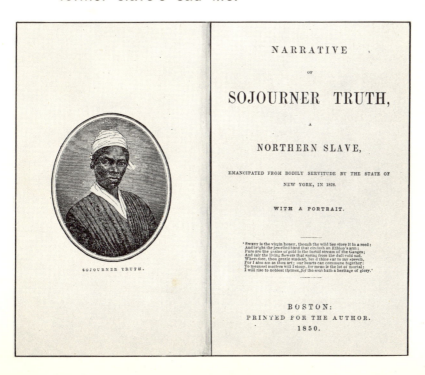

her book. People crowded around her to buy them.

One day, at a large outdoor meeting, the chairman called upon Sojourner to speak. As she stood up, it came to her that she would start by singing. She put all her strong feelings into the song she had made up:

I am pleading for my people,
A poor downtrodden race,
Who dwell in freedom's boasted land
With no abiding place.

Sojourner sang several verses, her voice ringing through the treetops. She then began to talk about the suffering of Mau-Mau Bett, Bomefree, and her son Peter. Tears rushed down the faces of many listeners.

The next winter Sojourner traveled

through New York State with a group of antislavery speakers. At the meetings Sojourner would sing and tell of the terrible life of the slaves.

"You are committing an awful sin by holding colored people in slavery. You don't know God, and God doesn't know you," Sojourner cried out to white Americans. "When I was a slave, I hated you. But now God has given me love enough so that I love even the white folks. Free my people and save yourselves from being punished by God."

The tour ended in Rochester. Sojourner spent the rest of the winter there with Amy Post, a friend of Olive Gilbert. Mrs. Post arranged meetings for Sojourner, who was now becoming well known as a speaker. She was the first black woman to give antislavery lectures in America.

7. Woman's Rights

In the spring Sojourner said good-bye to Mrs. Post. She left to give antislavery lectures in other parts of the country.

Sojourner traveled west. In May she was at Akron, Ohio. A woman's rights convention was being held there.

Sojourner had been told that women were beginning to make an organized fight for justice and equality. At that time a wife's earnings belonged to her husband. And by law their children belonged to him too. Few jobs were open to women, and they could not vote.

56

"We're trying to change these things," a white friend told Sojourner. "Women must have equal rights with men."

Sojourner agreed that women as well as blacks must win full human rights.

Sojourner walked into the convention at Akron and sat down on a step of the stage. The women in this midwestern city were upset. They feared that their cause would be hurt if it were connected with the antislavery movement, which was still unpopular in their part of the country. They did not want Sojourner to speak.

A number of ministers spoke, arguing against the women's movement. One shouted angrily, "God did not intend women to have equality with men!" Men in the audience clapped and roared their approval of the ministers' words.

Sojourner stood up then and began to

speak. "That man over there says that women need to be helped into carriages and lifted over ditches and to have the best place everywhere. Nobody ever helps me into carriages or over mud puddles or gives me any best place."

In a voice that sounded like rolling thunder, she asked, "And aren't I a woman?"

Sojourner bared her right arm to the shoulder and showed her muscles. "I have plowed and planted and gathered into barns, and no man could head me. And aren't I a woman?

"I could work as much and eat as much as a man when I could get it, and bear the lash as well. And aren't I a woman?"

Sojourner said that women were equal to men and should have the same rights. She spoke with humor and power. When

she finished, the applause was so loud that the windows rattled. "She . . . turned the whole tide in our favor," wrote the chairman.

All the rest of her life Sojourner was a fighter for woman's rights. She attended many woman's rights meetings and made wonderful speeches.

After the Akron convention, Sojourner stayed in Ohio. She worked for the freedom of the slaves. At first she spoke at meetings planned by antislavery groups. Then for a while she arranged her own meetings. Sojourner borrowed a horse and buggy and drove about alone.

When she came to a crossroads, she would lay down the reins and say, "God, you drive."

The horse would start down one of the roads. Sojourner told a friend, "We always came to some good place where I had a successful meeting."

It was not an easy life, though. White children often called Sojourner names and threw mud at her.

At one meeting a law student leaped to his feet. "Negroes are fit only to be slaves!" he shouted. "If any show intelligence, it's because they have white blood."

Sojourner held her head high. Around her hair, now gray, she wore a white turban in the African style. "I am pure African. You can all see that plain enough," she said with pride. "None of your white blood runs in my veins."

After two years in Ohio, Sojourner traveled back East. That autumn she visited Harriet Beecher Stowe, who lived in Andover, Massachusetts. Mrs. Stowe was the author of *Uncle Tom's Cabin*, a book that had turned many northerners against slavery.

From the first moment Mrs. Stowe was aware of Sojourner's great inner strength. Her home was full of guests whom she introduced to Sojourner. "No princess could have received a drawing-room with more composed dignity than Sojourner her audience," wrote Mrs. Stowe. "She stood among them, calm and erect, as one of her own native palm trees waving alone in the desert."

Mrs. Stowe realized that Sojourner's dignity was rare for a black of that time. Slavery stripped the dignity from men and women. Mrs. Stowe later wrote about Sojourner's visit for a magazine, *The Atlantic Monthly*. That article spread Sojourner's fame across the nation and to Europe.

8. Protest Against Slavery

Sojourner made her way back to the Middle West, where she lectured against slavery. The sale of her book brought money for her expenses.

Sojourner worked so hard that she began to look old and worn. Whenever she had to rest, she would stay for a short time with friends in Battle Creek, Michigan. She grew to like the town.

One day she told her friends, "I have enough money to start buying a little house. I believe I shall make my home here."

Perhaps her daughters would like to live in this pleasant place, she thought. She had never forgotten her dream that someday she would have a home where they all could be together. Her daughters were now over twenty-five and free. They were married, with families of their own. But they were poor, and life was hard for them.

Sojourner bought a small house. To her delight, one by one, her daughters with their husbands and children came to Battle Creek. They began setting up their own households; however, some members of the family always shared Sojourner's house.

Although she was now a homeowner, Sojourner kept on traveling and lecturing.

"Slavery must be destroyed, root and branch," she cried out to her audiences. More and more people in the North were against slavery.

In April 1861 the Civil War started. "Grant freedom to the slaves at once!" some abolitionists demanded. When President Lincoln failed to do this, they were angry.

"Have patience," advised Sojourner. "It takes a great while to turn around this great ship of state."

In January 1863 President Lincoln signed the Emancipation Proclamation. It freed the slaves in the rebellious Southern states. Sojourner's heart overflowed with joy. She sank to her knees and thanked God.

Just before Thanksgiving Day that year, Sojourner decided to bring a holiday

dinner to the black soldiers training near Detroit. Her friends in Battle Creek gladly helped prepare a feast.

On Thanksgiving Day Sojourner arrived at the army camp in a carriage. It was loaded with boxes of turkey, ham, mince pie, and nuts. While the feast was being set out for the eager soldiers, Sojourner started singing. She had made up words of her own to the tune of "John Brown's Body":

We are the hardy soldiers
* of the First of Michigan,*

We're fighting for the Union
* and for the rights of man,*

And when the battle rages,
* you'll find us in the van,*

As we go marching on.

9. A Talk
with President Lincoln

After the Emancipation Proclamation, Sojourner's thoughts turned to the problems of the newly freed black people. They were coming out of slavery just as she had, with no money and no schooling. They would need help in finding ways to live and support themselves. Did the nation understand this? Sojourner wondered.

The question came back to her over and over. One day in 1864 she made a decision. "I'll go talk with President Lincoln."

Sojourner reached Washington that fall.

She went to see Lucy Colman, an abolitionist friend. Mrs. Colman, a white woman, was now running some classes for black children in the city. She thought she could arrange an appointment with the president.

While she waited for the appointment, Sojourner walked around Washington. She was shocked at the awful misery she saw.

The city was crowded with 13,000 homeless blacks. After the proclamation, they had fled from the South and flocked to the capital. They lived in crowded neighborhoods. As many as 12 to 20 persons shared one-room windowless shacks.

Sojourner saw groups of men, their clothes in rags, leaning aimlessly against buildings. These men, who had worked on plantations, could find no jobs in the city.

She saw mothers, with babies clutched

in their arms, staring at one another in bewilderment. Some of the women still wore the old dresses of former mistresses.

Skinny little girls and boys searched through the garbage piled high in door-yards, looking for something to eat. The sight filled Sojourner with fear. She knew disease would spread rapidly in this filth.

Sojourner was now sixty-seven years old. But she realized there was new work for her to do. "I must stay in Washington and help these people," she decided.

Mrs. Colman was able to get an appointment with the president. She went with Sojourner to the White House and made the introduction. President Lincoln bowed and shook Sojourner's hand.

"I am pleased to see you," he said with a smile. "I have heard of you many times."

President Lincoln shows Sojourner his prized Bible.

"You are the best president who has ever taken the seat," Sojourner told him.

"I expect you have reference to my having emancipated the slaves in my proclamation," he said earnestly. "But President Washington and some of the other presidents would have done just as I have done, if the time had come."

Sojourner spoke warmly. "I thank God you were the instrument selected by Him and the people to do it."

President Lincoln opened a silver box and took out a Bible. On its gold cover was the picture of a slave with his chains falling from him. "This Bible was presented to me by the colored people of Baltimore," said the president.

"It's beautiful," exclaimed Sojourner, looking down at the Bible.

Then she raised her eyes and looked

directly at the president. "This government once sanctioned laws that would not permit my people to learn enough to enable them to read this book. And for what?" she protested.

A look of sadness came over the president's face.

He gladly signed Sojourner's "Book of Life." This was a book in which she collected signatures of people important to her. He wrote: "For Aunty Sojourner Truth, October 29, 1864. A. Lincoln."

The president shook Sojourner's hand when he said good-bye. "I will be pleased to have you call again," he said.

Walking away from the White House, Sojourner spoke thoughtfully to Mrs. Colman. "I felt that I was in the presence of a friend. I have faith that President Lincoln will take steps to help my people."

10. The Promise of Justice

Sojourner went to work in Freedmen's Village at Arlington, Virginia. This was across the Potomac River from Washington. Black people, still streaming into the capital area, were now sent to this new village. Life here was a little better than in the poor neighborhoods of Washington. Built on farmland, the village gave families small houses or rooms in barracks.

"We need you as a counselor," the superintendent of Freedmen's Village told Sojourner. Most of the women had a great deal to learn about homemaking. Like their husbands, they had worked on plantation fields from sunrise to dark.

"Be clean! Be clean! Cleanliness is godliness," Sojourner told the women as she walked from one house to another. She taught them how to cook and nurse the sick. And she talked with them about their children.

"Your children must go to school and learn to read," said Sojourner. "Then they can be somebody." The girls and boys eagerly went to classes taught by teachers from the North.

One day Sojourner came upon a group of weeping mothers. She learned that white men from Maryland had taken their children away. They made the children work for them without pay and kept them from school.

These residents of Freedmen's Village
pose in front of their drab barracks.

"Fight the robbers!" ordered Sojourner.
"You're free now. Don't let anyone treat
you like slaves. You have rights, and the
law will protect you." She helped the
mothers make use of the law to get their
children back.

One of the men from Maryland went to
Sojourner. "Old woman, stay out of our
affairs, or we'll put you in jail."

Sojourner glared at him. "If you try anything like that, I shall make the United States rock like a cradle," she snapped. The men left her alone.

As Sojourner carried on her work through the winter, it troubled her to see the large number of men without jobs. She learned, though, that they had bright hopes for the future. They counted on land in the South being given to them. Then they could be self-supporting.

"We blacks worked the land for more than two hundred years. Yet we don't own one inch of it, and we don't have a penny," one man told Sojourner. "President Lincoln isn't going to turn us loose like a bunch of stray dogs, with nothing."

"The government has promised forty acres and a mule to each family. The army officers told us that," said another man. He had fought with the Union army.

Sojourner believed the former slaves should have this land to give them a start. She trusted President Lincoln to help the blacks get what they needed.

That spring, on April 9, 1865, the war ended with victory for the Union. Six days later President Lincoln died from an assassin's bullet.

Stunned by their loss, the people of Freedmen's Village sobbed aloud in the streets. Sorrowfully they all draped their poor homes with black rags. Turning to Sojourner for comfort, they cried, "Mr. Lincoln was our savior."

Sojourner, her eyes filled with tears, nodded in agreement.

Andrew Johnson, who had been vice president, now became president. Sojourner decided she must see him. She asked Mrs.

Colman to arrange an appointment. On a Sunday afternoon Mrs. Colman once again went with Sojourner to the White House. She made the introduction.

"Please be seated, Mrs. Truth," said President Johnson.

"Sit down yourself, Mr. President," replied Sojourner politely. "I'm used to standing because I've been lecturing many years."

She spoke about her concern for the future of her people. President Johnson listened courteously. However, he did not say clearly what he planned to do to help black Americans.

11. Freedom Rides

Not long after this, the War Department asked Sojourner to work in Freedmen's Hospital in Washington. It was crowded with black men who had been wounded in the war. There was a serious shortage of nurses.

"I shall be glad to do all I can," Sojourner told the officials. She began her new work at once.

One morning she started for the hospital carrying a heavy sack of fruit. Suddenly she decided to take a streetcar.

When she first arrived in Washington, the horse-drawn streetcars were segregated. Special cars carried signs, saying "Colored Persons May Ride in This Car." Now the signs were gone. A law had been passed to forbid segregation on the streetcars. Blacks were shy, however, about claiming their right to ride in any streetcar they wanted.

Sojourner waved at a streetcar to stop. It went right by. Another streetcar came along, but the conductor paid no attention to Sojourner's signal.

"I want to ride!" she screamed. "I want to ride! I want to ride!"

Drivers stopped their carriages and their wagons to see what the cause of this excitement was. A traffic jam built up, forcing the streetcar to stop. Sojourner jumped in and took a seat.

The conductor glared at her. "Get outside and sit on the platform with the driver."

"I shall not," said Sojourner fearlessly. "I have paid five cents' fare, same as these other people. I intend to keep my seat."

"Do as I tell you or I'll throw you out!" roared the conductor.

"You better not try that, or I'll have the law on you," warned Sojourner. "I know my rights and you can't trample on them." The conductor turned away.

Sojourner was delighted with her victory. Later, walking up the path to the hospital, she promised herself, "I shall keep riding. Before I'm through, the conductors will change their ways."

A few days after that, Sojourner had to cross the city on an errand for the hospital. She waved at a streetcar, but it kept going. She ran after it as fast as she could. When the streetcar stopped to take on some white passengers, Sojourner leaped aboard.

She gasped, "It's a shame to make a lady run so."

The conductor said angrily, "I have a notion to throw you off."

Sojourner refused to back down. "If you try that, it will cost you more than your car and horses are worth," she cried. The conductor let her stay.

Several weeks later Sojourner battled again with the conductors. She and a white friend, Laura Haviland, had put in a hard day collecting supplies for the wounded black soldiers. Loaded with packages, they started for the hospital. Mrs. Haviland signaled a streetcar, and it stopped. Sojourner climbed quickly into the car.

"Get out of the way and let this lady come in," yelled the conductor.

"I am a lady too," said Sojourner.

He said no more. Soon Sojourner and Mrs. Haviland had to change to another streetcar. As they stepped in, a white passenger objected.

"Get off!" the conductor ordered harshly.

"I shall not," Sojourner answered. The conductor grabbed her shoulder.

"Don't put her out," said Mrs. Haviland.

The conductor asked angrily, "Does she belong to you?"

"No," replied Mrs. Haviland calmly. "She belongs to humanity."

"Then take her and go!" shouted the conductor. He slammed Sojourner against the door, but she refused to leave.

By the time she reached the hospital, she was in great pain. Physicians found that her shoulder had been badly hurt. Sojourner went to the police, and the conductor was arrested. He lost his job.

After that, conductors in Washington changed their ways. They stopped the streetcars to take on black people who wanted to ride.

12. Last Protest

Conditions at Freedmen's Hospital improved. So Sojourner decided to find out what she could do to help black refugees in the shacks in Washington. By now the government had opened soup houses in some of the poorest neighborhoods. Here parents stood in line to get food for their hungry families.

One winter day Sojourner went to a soup house. She saw a woman burst into tears. She had been handed one slice of bread and a quart of soup made from dried turnips and potatoes. "That's all the food I have for seven people," the woman wept. "My children are starving to death."

Sojourner visited this woman and her neighbors in their shacks. The shacks were freezing cold. Each family was allowed only two sticks of wood a day. Sojourner learned that in just one alley, four children had recently died.

Men sat around idle. "I'm so tired of doing nothing. It makes me feel no account," one man told Sojourner. The government had not given the forty acres and a mule that the freed slaves had counted on. There had been no distribution of land. The blacks felt cheated and discouraged.

"These people are being destroyed in body and spirit," thought Sojourner. "They must be helped to escape to a new way of life."

She prayed, "Show me the way, God."

An answer came to Sojourner. She thought of the land in the West owned by the federal government. Much of the land was still unsettled. She wanted the government to give it to the newly freed slaves and let them form communities there. The government should build houses, schools, and hospitals. It should give the men tools for farming, Sojourner decided. With this start, the black people could become self-supporting. They could learn how to manage their own affairs.

Sojourner had a friend write a paper that asked Congress to do these things. Then in February 1870 she traveled to Providence, Rhode Island. There, before a large group of white people, Sojourner told about the terrible conditions in Washington. She asked people to sign the paper she planned to send to Congress.

"Slavery kept my people poor. Give them land and a fair chance to work and get an education," pleaded Sojourner. "Do it and God will bless our country."

When Sojourner finished speaking, men and women pushed forward to sign the paper. After a few more meetings, Sojourner hurried back to Washington.

She delivered the petition to the United States Senate. Fifteen senators left their seats and came to the reception room to shake her hand. Later, one explained the Senate's view of what she asked. "It's an expensive program."

"This nation owes money to the empty-handed colored people for all their unpaid labor!" protested Sojourner.

"Congress will do what the majority of Americans demand," said the senator.

90

"Then I shall go stir up a majority," said the spirited lady of seventy-three.

Carrying many copies of the petition, Sojourner left Washington. She began lecture tours throughout the North and the Middle West. Her grandson Sammy Banks, a young man of twenty, went with her. To help pay their way, she sold photographs of herself.

At her meetings Sojourner asked people to back her program to help the suffering blacks. After hearing her moving talk, most listeners willingly put their names on the paper. Friends along the way took charge of sending copies to Congress. Sojourner dreamed of getting so many signatures that Congress would have to act.

After a while her audiences became smaller, however. Sojourner had to face

Sojourner sold this picture of herself to pay the costs of her trips. The poster below announces one of her lectures.

FREE LECTURE!

SOJOURNER TRUTH,

Who has been a slave in the State of New York, and who has been a Lecturer for the last twenty-three years, whose characteristics have been so vividly portrayed by Mrs. Harriet Beecher Stowe, as the African Sybil, will deliver a lecture upon the present issues of the day,

At   On

And will give her experience as a Slave mother and religious woman. She comes highly recommended as a public speaker, having the approval of many thousands who have heard her earnest appeals, among whom are Wendell Phillips, Wm. Lloyd Garrison, and other distinguished men of the nation.

☞ At the close of her discourse she will offer for sale her photograph and a few of her choice songs.

the fact that most Americans wanted to forget the problems of the blacks.

"You don't care about colored people, but God does. They are going to be a people among you!" Sojourner cried out to white Americans.

Her lonely, heroic fight to force Congress to help her people ended after four years. Sammy fell ill, and they returned to Battle Creek where this beloved grandson died. Sojourner herself became very ill, but her daughters nursed her back to health.

In her last years Sojourner went on speaking for the rights of women and black Americans. In one year alone she lectured in 36 towns in Michigan. "Stretch out your hand in brotherhood to the colored people," she begged her white listeners. "We are all the children of one Father in heaven."

In 1883, when Sojourner was eighty-six years old, she was stricken with a fatal illness. Her daughters took care of her in her home at Battle Creek. "I have done the best I could," Sojourner murmured to them toward the end. Though she was in great pain, a light filled her face.

Sojourner whispered, "I have told the whole truth."

Index